Weapons Of Righteousness

Weapons Of Righteousness

by Alden Reed

© Copyright 1993 —Alden Reed

All rights reserved. This book is protected under the copyright laws of the United States of America. This book may not be copied or reprinted for commercial gain or profit. Short quotations or occasional page copying for personal or group study is permitted and encouraged. Permission will be granted upon request. Unless otherwise identified, Scripture quotations are from The New American Standard Version of the Bible.

Take note that the name satan and related names are not capitalized. We choose not to acknowledge him, even to the point of violating grammatical rules.

Treasure House
a division of
Destiny Image
P.O. Box 310
Shippensburg, PA 17257-0310

ISBN 1-56043-751-0

For Worldwide Distribution
Printed in the U.S.A.

Destiny Image books are available through these fine distributors outside the United States:

Christian Growth, Inc., Jalan Kilang-Timor, Singapore 0315	Successful Christian Living Capetown, Rep. of South Africa
Lifestream Nottingham, England	Vision Resources Ponsonby, Auckland, New Zealand
Rhema Ministries Trading Randburg, South Africa	WA Buchanan Company Geebung, Queensland, Australia
Salvation Book Centre Petaling, Jaya, Malaysia	Word Alive Niverville, Manitoba, Canada

Dedication

To my heavenly Father,
To my Lord Jesus Christ,
To my Teacher, the Holy Spirit,
Also to my Helpmate, my sons and daughters,
and to the ministry to which God has called me.

My thanks to my mom, Frances, for her devotion to Jesus and her many hours of labor on transcribing this book from tape;

my wife and helpmate, Connie (she is also my best friend);

my 15-year-old son, Luke, for his labor in our ministry; and

Joetta and Jodi for their many hours of typing, editing and laboring in love.

Contents

Chapter		Page
1	A Vendetta in Christ	1
2	He Who Is Weak in Soul...Dies	5
3	Gifts and Character of the Holy Spirit	15
4	Love—The Foundational Weapon	19
5	The Weapon of Peace	23
6	The Weapon of Gentleness	27
7	The Strength of Joy	31
8	The Weapon of Goodness	35
9	The Consistent Power of Faithfulness	39
10	The Battle Zone of Self-Control	47
11	Patience and Kindness	51
12	Jesus-Breathed Power Is Forgiveness	55
13	Warrior Sons and Daughters of God	63
	Summary	67
	About the Author	69

Notes

Chapter One
A Vendetta in Christ

An insatiable drive to be somebody special, to be able to do something nobody else could do was the driving power that on several occasions nearly ended my life. Even coming close to death became a thrilling experience instead of a sobering one. By the time I was eighteen I had been arrested twenty times in one year for street racing. Finally a judge gave me the choice: go to prison or join the Army. I took the second choice and served my country for the next three years. During that time I did more racing than ever before, but this time it was at a near-by drag strip. But my desire to be the best was never satisfied, even breaking a national record the thrill only lasted a day. What could I do next and next. The Rolling Stones record of "Can't Get No Satisfaction" became my theme song. I would listen to it many times a day.

Not long after my discharge from the Army, I decided to attempt to set a new water skiing world record of 125 miles per hour on one ski. During a practice session on a narrow river, however, I suffered a serious accident which left me laying bleeding on the bank for several long and painful hours. During the days and weeks that followed, a spirit of fear took hold of me. Eventually this fear reduced me to a pathetic emotional and mental wreck.

To cope with the ever-present fear and mental anguish, I began using drugs. This quickly began to effect my marriage. In her own attempt to tolerate me, and the things in her own life she couldn't seem to change, my wife began using drugs herself. Then in 1975 at the age of twenty-eight, she committed suicide.

Shortly after my first wife's death, I married my present wife, Connie. Through a string of unusual events, my new wife and I gave our lives to Jesus Christ. Since that time I have grown in the love of this new relationship with Christ. His perfect love has cast out all my fears and brought healing and deliverance to my once troubled mind, and has given me a great sense of peace, a real satisfaction and contentment.

Thrilled to be "free" after eight long years of being in bondage to fear, I began to study and pray almost constantly for an entire year. At the end of this time, God called me to preach His gospel. Connie and I studied with the Assemblies of God and then attended Lester Sumrall's World Harvest Bible College where I received my ministerial degree.

During the time when we were preparing for the ministry, two of our sons were killed when the car they were in collided with a train. Out of this tragedy, born within me was a personal "vendetta in Christ" against the works of the devil. Some may ask, was the devil responsible for the death of our sons. Isn't life and death in the hands of the Lord? John 10:10 plainly states, "the devil has come to steal, kill and destroy." It is through spiritual ignorance that men say things like, "well, God needed two more roses in heaven." Death is an enemy of the Christian, according to God's Word, death is not the ultimate escape but the ultimate enemy. Paul declared, "For He (Jesus) must reign until He has put all His enemies under His feet. The last enemy to be destroyed is death" (I Cor. 15:25,26). Nor is death the end of our human existence. The Bible declares, "Man is destined to die once, and after that to face judgment" (Hebrews 9:27). Apart from salvation through faith in the Lord Jesus Christ, death is the doorway to eternal suffering. I began to search the Scriptures looking for the key to obtaining God's power—that is, His power to destroy the works of the evil one. I sought for power; I preached power; I became desperate for the power to tear down the devil's strongholds, bring deliverance, and set the captives free. As a result of this determined search for God's power, I discovered something I had not expected—the necessity of God's holiness.

When I speak of holiness, I am not speaking from a detached theological point of view; I am talking about the holiness that flows out of a personal relationship with the risen Son of God, Jesus Christ, who causes old things to pass away and all things to become new—to become holy. This is not a legalistic holiness; it is the holiness that shines from those who have been transformed into the image of the "Holy One of God."

I have heard little talk about the fruit of the Holy Spirit in recent years. But in this last hour, the fruit of the Holy Spirit (a phrase which I consider to be synonymous with conformity to the image and character of Jesus) must be manifest within every believer. As I have sought the Lord for His power, He has shown me that there is great power in the fruit of the Holy Spirit. It is an individual power within the life of each believer. But it comes only to those who have an intimate, personal relationship with Christ and His Spirit. Many have sought the power of God in many places and in many ways, but a personal, intimate relationship with Jesus Christ is the *only* way, for He is "The Way." This relationship is how God will raise up holy and powerful men and women of God, fully equipped to fight a holy war.

Chapter 2

He Who Is Weak in Soul...Dies

If I made the statement that Jesus Christ was crucified because of His weakness, many believers would rise up and cry, "No, not so!" But is this not what the Scripture says? Second Corinthians 13:4 states, "For indeed He was crucified because of weakness, yet He lives because of the power of God." Jesus was crucified "because of weakness." This is not to say that Jesus was weak. As a man, He had the heart and will of a fighter. He had the grit and guts of an endurance runner who would not quit or turn back. The adversary could not take Him even though he tried many times. It was not until Jesus surrendered His will to the Father that His mission could be completed, then and only then was the enemy finally able to take Him captive (Luke 22:42). Had Jesus not surrendered His will, no force would have been able to take Him.

Please do not misunderstand, Jesus was submitted to His Father, but yet He said, "Father, if Thou art willing, remove this cup from Me; Yet not My will but

Thine be done." (Luke 22:42) What I am trying to say is there came a time when He surrendered His will to fight the powers of darkness and then He was taken. (Luke 22:53) "While I was with you daily in the temple, you did not lay hands on Me; but this hour and the power of darkness are yours."

Jesus Christ had the will, the heart, and the soul of a fighter. I believe God's people need that same mindset. Some of you may be tired of fighting, but beloved, if you quit, you lose. It is not your spirit that is tired; it is your soul. We must rise up and be strong-willed, strong-hearted, and strong-minded in Christ.

The apostle Paul wrote the following exhortation to the believers in Ephesus:

Finally, be strong in the Lord, and in the strength of His might. Put on the full armor of God, that you may be able to stand firm against the schemes of the devil. For our struggle is not against flesh and blood, but against the rulers, against the powers, against the world forces of darkness, against spiritual forces of wickedness in the heavenly places. Therefore, take up the full armor of God, that you may be able to resist in the evil day and having done everything, to stand firm (Ephesians 6:10-18).

Now, hear what the Spirit says: "This armor does not protect your spirit. This armor is designed to protect your soul. For it is the soul of man that this war is over."

You may ask, "If the Spirit of Jesus Christ is in me, can the devil capture that Spirit?" No, he certainly cannot. What is he after then? The answer is your soul. *This includes your mind, your will, your heart, and your conscience. These are what make up your soul,* and your soul is what the thief of darkness is after.

If you are a born-again believer, then the Spirit that lives in you is the same Spirit that lives in other believers. In that Spirit, we are all equal. Even young children, in the Spirit, are equal with adults. Young believers do not have a child Holy Spirit; they have the entire Holy Spirit. What is the difference then between the immature believer and the mature believer? It is in the soul—the mind, the will, the heart, and the conscience. If one believer is weaker than another, it is due to a weakness of the soul. If one believer is stronger than another, it is simply because the strong believer is more yielded to the Holy Spirit. This yieldedness to the Spirit will bring a mind closer to conformity to the mind of Christ; it will bring a will closer to conformity to the will of the Father. The stronger, more mature believer should manifest more grit, more heart and more soul. He should be able to stand more firm-in-the-faith than the weaker brother.

The Holy Spirit is constantly working to transform every believer into the image and character of Jesus Christ, with the grit to stand against the adversary. But there is a war going on and many believers do not know what it's all about. I'll tell you what it's all about: it's about your soul!

The Bible tells the story of a man who said, "I've got it all. My soul is prosperous. I can just lay back." But the Lord said, "Today your soul is required of you." We are all accountable to God for the condition of our soul. As believers in a holy God, we are responsible for monitoring what we see, hear, read and watch. Many in the Body of Christ are busy polluting their own souls. Rather than communing with the trash of this world, we ought to be communing with the holy One of Heaven. It's no wonder that so many of us feel that damnable war going on inside us so much of the time. We are committing spiritual suicide by helping the enemy to destroy our own souls.

One of the great sins of both David and Solomon was that they allowed their eyes to feast on the wrong things. But Jesus said, "And if your eye causes you to stumble, pluck it out, and throw it from you. It is better for you to enter life with one eye, than having two eyes, to be cast into fiery hell" (Matt. 18:9). What we feast on with our eyes goes down into our souls where it works either for our good or our ill. We must keep our eyes from causing our souls to be polluted with filth and wickedness. Some may be stumbling because of what they are allowing into their souls through their eyes.

David wrote, "He restores my soul" (Psalms 23:3). The Holy Spirit is not trying to kill your soul; He is trying to restore it. If your soul resists the Holy Spirit and does not allow Him to work, it just could resist itself into serious trouble at the coming of Christ. Jesus said He would spit the lukewarm right out of His mouth. Beloved, it is not the spirit that is lukewarm, but the soul.

Some readers may think of Romans 12:11, "be fervent in spirit" and ask therefore if lukewarmness isn't a problem of the spirit. According to Strongs Concordance, the Greek word here for spirit is also the same word for mind or mental disposition, and the American Dictionary definition for fervent is, "having or showing great warmth and earnestness of feeling." I believe we can see that Romans Scrpiture is speaking of our Christian responsibility to society; this responsibility and our actions are manifest actions of our soul (mind, will, heart).

Holiness in the life of a believer is a serious matter to God. Your soul is the real you. Your born-again spirit will return to God, but will the real you go with it? We have been bought and paid for by the precious blood of Jesus Christ. We are no longer our own to do as we please. God will not play games with those who count the blood of Jesus Christ a cheap thing. As James wrote, we must "submit therefore to God. Resist the devil and he will flee from you" (James 4:7). The devil is only compelled to flee from those who are submitted to God.

Who is it that will ascend to the hill of the Lord? Is it everyone who professes belief in Christ? David writes that it is "He who has clean hands and a pure heart, who has not lifted up his soul to falsehood, and has not sworn deceitfully. He shall receive a blessing from the Lord" (Psalms 24:4-5). This Scripture speaks of holiness. It describes the character of Jesus Christ and the character of those who are truly submitted to Him. This is the character that results in the spiritual power that treads upon serpents and over all the power of the enemy.

In light of Psalm 24, can you see how damaging the pollution of this world is when we put it into our souls? The sex, the violence, and the mockery of good that is pumped into our homes through the television damns and pollutes the souls of God's own people. The places we go, the things we do, the people we hang with— these things either bring blessing or cursing to our souls. There is no grey area. No wonder this damnable war continuously rages within so many of us.

The body just stands there awaiting its orders. It normally does only what the soul tells it to do. If the soul is not in submission to the Spirit and is not conformed to the character of Christ, the body will do the wrong thing again and again. When the soul is in unity with the Holy Spirit, then we will become true Christians, doing Christ-like things by nature.

David wrote, "As the deer pants for the water brooks, so my soul pants for Thee, O God" (Psalms 42:1). God created the soul with the capability to "pant" for God. That is one reason why the devil is out to capture it. He wants your soul to pant after him, or the things of this world—anything but after God.

The world of the occult is filled with demonic strategies designed to capture the soul—E.S.P., soul travel, meditation of the mind, yoga, mind reading, and the list goes on. But God has provided us with weapons of righteousness that are mightier than anything the devil can come up with.

II Corinthians 6:1-7 can be summed up by saying, "And working together with Him, as servants of God, in purity, in knowledge, in patience, in kindness, in the Holy Spirit, and genuine love, in the word of truth, in the power of God; by the weapons of righteousness for the right hand and the left." We can certainly see the fruit of the Holy Spirit present if we are really at work together with Him.

When we are born again we become Christ-like in the Spirit. That is why the Bible says that in the Spirit we are all equal, male and female, Jew and Gentile, rich and poor. But in the soul it is our responsibility to be submissive to the work of the Holy Spirit. My prayer for myself is, "Lord, do whatever is necessary to conform me to the image of Jesus, that my heart would be like His, my will would be that of the Father's, and my mind would be the mind of Christ."

In the intellect of the natural mind, it is impossible to separate the soul and the spirit. Hebrews 4:12 says, "For the word of God is living and active and sharper than any two-edged sword, and piercing as far as the division of soul and spirit." It is only the word of God that can tell us what is of the spirit of man and what is of the soul.

"My soul waits in silence for God only; from Him is my salvation. He only is my rock and my salvation, my stronghold; I shall not be greatly shaken" (Psalms 62:1-2). When our soul is submitted to the Spirit of God, when we stop polluting it, then the Holy Spirit will produce His fruit; that is, the character traits of Jesus in us. And it is only then that we will have more Christ-like power.

"O God, Thou art my God; I shall seek Thee earnestly; my soul thirsts for Thee, my flesh yearns for Thee, in a dry and weary land where there is no water" (Psalms 63:1). Beloved, the Word of God is our food and the Spirit of God is our drink in this dry and weary world. The Scriptures are the manna from Heaven and the Holy Spirit is the drink. We must stop eating and drinking the spiritual junk food of this world.

Behind every power in our society, behind all the worldly systems, there lies a coiled power. To the degree that a believer puts his hand into this world system and partakes of it, to that degree he communes with the power of the adversary. Many of us have polluted our souls for far too long. We now find ourselves living in a dry and weary land. We need to immediately begin partaking on the Bread of Heaven and the Water of Life, that our souls would be transformed into the image of Christ.

Because our enemy is a spiritual being, our weapons and our armour must also be spiritual. Paul writes, "Therefore, take up the full armour of God, that you may be able to resist in the evil day, and having done everything, to stand firm. Stand firm therefore, having girded your loins with truth, and having put on the breastplate of righteousness, and having shod your feet with the preparation of the gospel of peace; in addition to all, taking up the shield of faith with which you will be able to extinguish all the flaming missiles of the evil one. And take the helmet of salvation, and the sword of the Spirit, which is the word of God" (Eph. 6:13-17). This Scripture reveals that the armor of God is designed to protect the soul of man: the helmet protects the mind; the breastplate protects the heart and the seat of the will; the belt of truth, which Peter said we should use to gird up the loins of our minds: feet shod with the preparation of the gospel of peace. The shield of faith and the Sword are the offensive weapons as compared to the other pieces which are defensive. Faith is simply "Trust" and in this trusting will be our calm, and our confidence which in turn will keep our hearts from failing because of fear. Of course the Sword is the Word of God. The Psalmist said hide the Word in your heart and you would not sin against God. This sword is also our authority in Christ, so be careful who you swing it at, it does have the power to kill. Once when I was preaching in a penitentiary a converted convict said to me, "they that live by the sword shall die by the sword." He said the Holy Spirit had shown him that Christians who use their Father's Word to cut up their own brothers would be in serious trouble at the judgment seat of Christ. We are to walk in the straight path of holiness unto the Lord, taking faith in one hand and the sword in the other, going out as Christ-like warriors to overcome and conquer, our souls standing firm because we have the grit, the guts, and the heart of a winner!

Notes

Chapter 3

Gifts and Character of the Holy Spirit

Year after year, as I have pursued my vendetta in Christ to destroy the works of the devil, the Holy Spirit has continued to remind me of First Corinthians 13:1-2, which states, "If I speak with the tongues of men and of angels, but do not have love, I have become a noisy gong or a clanging cymbal. And if I have the gift of prophecy, and know all mysteries and all knowledge; and if I have all faith, so as to remove mountains, but I do not have love, I am nothing." The powerful gifts of God's Spirit are only powerless "noise" when used apart from His character—that is, His love. God forbid that the Church would continue just making noise. It is time for the men and women of God to rise up in submission to the Holy Spirit and be transformed into the image and character of the Lord Jesus Christ.

In First Corinthians 12:1, Paul writes, "Now concerning spiritual gifts, brethren, I do not want you to be unaware." And then in verses 4-10 he writes, "Now there are varieties of gifts, but the same Spirit. And there are varieties of ministries, and the same Lord. And there are varieties of effects, but the same God who works all things in all persons. But to each one is given the manifestation of the Spirit for the common good. For to one is given the word of wisdom through the Spirit, and to another the word of knowledge according to the same Spirit; to another faith by the same Spirit, and to another gifts of healing by the one Spirit, and to another the effecting of miracles, and to another prophecy, and to another the distinguishing of spirits, to another the various kinds of tongues, and to another the interpretation of tongues." And then in verse 31 of the same chapter, Paul writes, "And I show you a still more excellent way." Notice that in the verses from Chapter 13 Paul named five of the spiritual gifts which he had just listed in chapter 12. But notice something absolutely essential to living the true spirit-empowered life: five "gifts" of the Spirit are listed, but only one portion of the ninefold "fruit" of the Spirit is named. Paul then makes an awesome statement that many Spirit-filled believers have overlooked: without the fruit of the Holy Spirit, the gifts of the Holy Spirit are only noise! The five supernatural power-gifts can be completely disempowered by the absence of one-ninth of the Holy Spirit's fruit.

The fruit of the Holy Spirit is the character of Jesus Christ. When the character of Christ and the gifts of His Spirit work together, then we will see the manifestation of the true power of God in our lives.

Though most of us truly do desire the fruit of the Holy Spirit to be produced in our lives, there is one tragic mistake that we seem to make over and over again. We can not produce this fruit ourselves no matter how hard we try. This fruit is of the Holy Spirit, and only He can produce it. Our part is to submit to the work He is doing in us on a day-by-day, moment-by-moment basis.

Paul declared, "It is no longer I who live, but Christ lives in me" (Gal. 2:20). We must decrease, and allow Christ to increase within our souls. Christ Himself is the fruit. Paul wrote that he travailed until Christ was "formed" in the believers (Gal. 4:19). Let us comprehend before God that in our experience there is neither thing nor affair, but only Christ. It is not that He leads the way, but that He *is* the Way; not that He gives us light, but that He *is* the Light; not that He teaches us the truth, but that He *is* the Truth; not that He gives us peace, but that He *is* Peace; not that He gives us love; but that He *is* Love, not that He gives us life, but that He *is* our Life. I pray that we can all grasp the difference here. What Christ gives us is not just His gifts; it is Himself. When we truly have Him, we have all that He is.

The Bread of Life is a thing, so also is the light, the way, the truth, peace and love. But in Christianity we ought not be concerned about acquiring things—only Christ! The fruit of the Holy Spirit in your life is not the acquisition of things; it is the Holy Spirit forming Christ in us. Therefore, our submission to the Holy Spirit is so that He may bring forth Christ in our character more and more until we can also say, "It is no longer I who live, but it is Christ who lives within me."

My intention is not to write about formulas or methods, for only Christ living in us produces true spiritual power. Even if a person learned an entire set of biblical methods, he would not then be educated into being a Christian—God's children are born, not taught. Everything spiritual outside of Jesus Christ is dead. In salvation, the way to Heaven is Christ Himself. There is no formula outside of Him that can get a person inside the Pearly Gates. We must see that the Lord Jesus is the only way by which we can come to God. This is true both at the first moment of salvation, and also at any other subsequent time in our Christian experience. God has not given us things, methods or formulas; He has given us His Son.

The fruit of the Holy Spirit can only be produced in us as we make contact with the Lord through "living faith." We cannot touch the Lord through some "copied faith formula." A method has no power, since no matter how good it may seem to be, since it is not Christ, it is simply a dead thing. The true character of Christ in your life can only come through experience with the true Christ. Anything else produces only a counterfeit—a dead thing.

Chapter 4

Love—The Foundational Weapon

When Paul listed the attributes of the fruit of the Holy Spirit, the first thing on the list was love. I believe that in a sense it is the only fruit, and that everything else on the list is but a manifestation of the fruit of love. These manifestations of love are described as follows:

> Joy is love's "strength."
> Peace is love's "security."
> Patience is love's "waiting."
> Kindness is love's "humility."
> Goodness is love's "character."
> Faithfulness is love's "confidence."
> Gentleness is love's "conduct."
> Self-control is love's "victory."

The devil cannot counterfeit the fruit of the Holy Spirit. There is no love in him, neither is there any peace, joy, or kindness. He is, however, capable of counterfeiting the gifts of the Spirit, including miraculous signs and wonders. This is a good reason why we should not put our seal of approval on a ministry just because of the demonstration of power gifts. Rather than looking for gifts, we ought to be examing the ministries around us for fruit.

Jesus warned, "Beware of the false prophets, who come to you in sheep's clothing" (Matt. 7:15). They may look and talk like sheep, but that's not enough. According to the Lord, inwardly they may be "ravenous wolves." The only true indicator of authentic Christian discipleship is spiritual fruit. A good tree cannot bear bad fruit, and a bad tree cannot bear good fruit. Every one carrying a Bible is not necessarily a man of God. We must look for the fruit in the minister's life, and the number one fruit must be love.

I counseled a young woman several years ago who failed to look for the fruit of the Holy Spirit in the life of the young man she intended to marry. She came to my office one afternoon and told me that she had met this man. She loved him very much, but he was unsaved. I counseled her that she should not have gotten so involved with an unbeliever. He did agree to meet with me though and on two occasions I shared Christ with him. On our second meeting he prayed to accept Christ as his Savior. I then privately instructed the young woman to wait at least three months and watch to see if the fruit of the Holy Spirit began to appear.

She waited two days. Then, contrary to my counsel, she found a preacher who would marry them immediately. Three days after the marriage, she called me and asked me to help her get a divorce. Needless to say, I was shocked.

Through the pain and tears of a broken heart, she told me what had happened. Immediately after the wedding, she said, this man had taken her to Chicago where they spent the night in a motel. The first thing the next morning he had taken her to a high-rise building but would not tell her what he was doing. While she waited he spoke to a man behind a counter, who seemed to be preparing some papers. He then called for her. The clerk instructed her to sign her name on one of the papers. When she asked what she was signing, he replied that it was her husband's immigration papers. Since he had married an American citizen, he could now become a permanent resident.

She suddenly realized that she was only being used by this man she had married. With tears streaming down her cheeks, she ran out of the office and into the hall. Her new supposedly Christian husband quickly caught up with her and took her aside. He pulled a snub-nosed revolver from under his jacket and told her that she was to go back in and sign those papers or else! In a sudden blast of fury, this young, wounded woman smashed him in the face with her fist. With that she turned and ran out of the building and out of his life.

We could not get a local judge to decree an annulment because the marriage had been "sexually consummated." The woman had to borrow $250.00 for the divorce and then, nine months later, she gave birth to the child of a bad memory. If only this young woman had waited to see if the fruit of God's Spirit had become evident in the life of this man she so desperately wanted to marry, she would have spared herself much pain and shame. We learned later that he was a Mexican drug smuggler and had bragged about how he was going to get an American girl to marry him so he could cross the border easier.

Let's examine the power of the fruit of love. The most menacing and destructive spiritual enemy most of us face is fear and its companion torment. It is the adversaries greatest weapon. Fear comes disguised in many other names. For example, jealousy is the fear of someone taking a loved one from you. Worry is the fear of not having enough money to pay your bills. Anxiety is the fear of what may happen to you in the future. Selfishness is the fear of not getting enough of something for yourself. Shyness is the fear of being rejected by other people. The lack of self-confidence is the fear of failure. Insecurity is the fear of not being taken care of. Many other names are rooted in fear, which is a major destroyer of faith and a sound mind.

Love is the most potent weapon against fear. The Bible says, "Perfect love casts out fear" (I John 4:18). The love of God takes the devil by the throat and casts him and his fear out of our lives.

Jesus said, "Love your enemies" (Matt. 5:44). Paul put it this way, "But if your enemy is hungry, feed him" (Romans 12:20). How could this be? It is because love is not afraid of the enemy. Fear wants to destroy the enemy so he can no longer cause pain. But love is much more powerful than fear. Love not only is not afraid of the enemy, but love is even willing to strengthen the enemy and still not be afraid of him. Love is confident and secure in the Father's provisions and protection.

This "perfect love" that casts out fear comes into our lives through our pursuit of a growing personal relationship with the One Who is Perfect Love.

This kind of love is the foundational weapon of the weapons of righteousness and is mightier than anything the adversary has ever even imagined.

Chapter 5

The Weapon of Peace

Peace may be the most aggressive of all the weapons of righteousness. During the times when I have walked in the greatest peace with the Lord, I have also been the most unmanageable by the adversary. The devil motivates and manipulates God's people by promoting worry and fear in the face of difficult situations. The peace of God in my life cancels out these destructive forces.

There are twenty-seven books in the New Testament. Twenty-one of them either begin or end with words to this effect: "May the grace and peace of God be with you." Peace is sought after by more people in this world than perhaps anything else. Peace conferences are held around large tables where men negotiate over how best to establish peace in their lands. Men seek for peace with other nations, peace in their homes, peace with their relatives, peace with other people, and peace with God. Romans 12:18 says, "If possible, so far as it depends on you, be at peace with all men." Mark 9:50 says, "Be at peace with one another." Matthew 5:9 says, "Blessed are the peacemakers, for they shall be called the sons of God."

The world searches for peace in many ways and in many places, but there is only one place where it can be found—in the Prince of Peace. Jesus Christ does not just give peace, He is peace. In Luke 7:50 Jesus said, "Your faith has saved you; go in peace." Peace is inherent in the person and character of Jesus Christ.

The work of the Holy Spirit is the developing of the character traits of Jesus in us so that we can be like Him in this present life. He is working on us, in us, and through us. He is trying to lead us out of a lifestyle that is dominated by our flesh and into a lifestyle that is dominated by His leadership. Rest assured, brothers and sisters, He will never stop working in your life. The Holy Spirit is able to lead us in every detail of life, but I believe this will only happen for those who allow Him to carry on His character-building work within their souls.

The Holy Spirit is not working just to give us temporary victories, but rather that we would become Christ-like victors. To be a victor you need the heart of a winner, which is the character of Christ.

A believer with abiding peace in his heart can overcome fear, regardless of what that fear may be. Fear of death, for example, can be completely overcome by peace. How many elderly believers have given powerful witness to the reality of God as they faced imminent death with utmost peace.

As the fruit of peace has ripened in my life under the watchful care of the Holy Spirit, I have become more and more unmanageable by the devil. Christians need not be afraid of every dire situation that comes along. Anguish here and torment there, trying situations and circumstances—these are open doors for demonic activity. Many Christians are allowing themselves to be vulnerable before the devil. The peace of Jesus Christ will change you from being vulnerable into an aggressive soldier wielding this devil-defeating weapon of righteousness.

Because of peace, the devil could do nothing to manipulate Jesus. He faced death with perfect peace. There was no kicking and screaming as they led Him to the cross. He could not be turned from His purpose, because the peace of God was resident in His heart.

Have you ever tried to hear the voice of the Holy Spirit while you were in the midst of an anxiety attack? It is undiscernable. The best way to hear His voice is when there is peace and calm in your heart. This fruit is vitally important to every believer. The Holy Spirit leads us by an inner witness which is much easier to discern when peace is reigning. When a believer hears a wrong doctrine or is in some kind of a hazardous position, the Holy Spirit will many times trouble our spirit so as to arouse an alertness within us. If you are already troubled because you lack peace, you will be unable to discern the Holy Spirit's warning. The enemy will try to overpower the peace that God gives with his overpowering voice of fear and worry.

God our Father is interested in His children's concerns. To walk in intimate fellowship with Him is the secret to receiving His peace. Once we truly comprehend the fatherhood of God, there will be supernatural inner peace that surpasses all understanding. As believers we need to seek after the fruit of peace. Remember, it is found only in an intimate, personal relationship with the Prince of Peace Himself.

If you desire to walk in the Spirit and be lead by His inner witness, then you must make learning about the fruit of the Holy Spirit and the character of Jesus Christ a top priority. How many times do you think the sick, the lame and the brokenhearted came to Jesus and He said, "Not right now. You will disturb my peace"? Not once! Peace is not something you do; it is something you become through Jesus Christ.

Psalms 34:14 says, "Seek peace, and pursue it." We must pursue God's peace because it is the atmosphere into which the voice of the Holy Spirit speaks. Ephesians 2:14 says that Jesus Christ Himself "is our peace." This peace is available to us now. Let us allow the Holy Spirit to ripen it in our lives. The devil can't make you or shake you; he can't motivate you, and he can't overcome you, when you live and walk in the peace of Jesus Christ.

Chapter 6

The Weapon of Gentleness

Matthew 5:5 reads, "Blessed are the gentle, for they shall inherit the earth." Immediately following Paul's listing of the fruit of the Holy Spirit in Galatians 5:22 and 23, we are given an example in chapter six as to how to use the fruit of gentleness. Paul writes, "If a man is caught in any trespass, you who are spiritual, restore such a one in a spirit of gentleness" (Gal. 6:1). We are to treat our brothers and sisters in love even when they sin. Out of the fruit of love, the conduct of gentleness comes forth.

Gentleness is love's conduct. It is one of the greatest characteristics of Christian manhood. A Christian man can be tough, he can be strong, he can be bold, he can be firm, he can even exercise authority and power, but without gentleness he falls short of the character of Jesus Christ.

Gentleness is also one of the greatest qualities of a Christian woman. I Peter 3:1 says, "In the same way, you wives, be submissive to your own husbands so that even if any of them are disobedient to the word, they may be won without a word by the behavior of their wives; as they observe your chaste and respectful behavior". Now, Peter doesn't just stop there; he goes on to speak of the hidden person of the heart: "and let not your adornment be merely external...but let it be the hidden person of the heart, with the imperishable quality of a gentle and quiet spirit, which is precious in the sight of God." Shouldn't every Christian woman want to possess that which is "precious" in the sight of our Lord?

I believe that all Christian men should be known as "gentle-men." The apostle Paul said, "But I will come to you soon, if the Lord wills, and I shall find out, not the words of those who are arrogant, but their power" (I Corinthians 4:19). There are some in the Church who have lots of words but no power. As the saying goes, talk is cheap. But Paul went on to say, "For the Kingdom of God does not consist in words but in power" (I Corinthians 4:20). Contrary to the ways of the world, the power of God is manifested most dynamically through the spirit of gentleness, which is the opposite of harsh arrogance.

Gentleness would not only stop most fights and arguments in churches, but also most fights and arguments in homes. The gentle spirit will bring forth the "soft answer" that turns away wrath. It will leave an open door for the Holy Spirit to enter. Therefore, gentleness becomes a mighty weapon in the life of an obedient Christian. Let us be reminded, "the weapons of our warfare are not of the flesh, but divinely powerful for the destruction of fortresses" (I Corinthians 10:4).

Though we are in fleshly bodies we do not war according to the flesh. Any believer who develops the character of Jesus Christ, the fruit of the Holy Spirit, becomes a warrior wielding the weapons of God's own righteousness. These weapons have great power to overcome the contradictions and fears implanted in the hearts and minds of men by satan himself.

In Matthew 11:29 Jesus said, "Learn from Me, for I am gentle and humble in heart; and you shall find rest for your souls". The most powerful being in the universe says, "I am gentle and humble in heart." As believers, we must have this quality of Jesus in our lives.

First Peter 3:15 states, "But sanctify Christ as Lord in your hearts, always being ready to make a defense to everyone who asks you to give an account for the hope that is in you, yet with gentleness and reverence." Whenever we speak, we should speak with gentleness, especially when proclaiming Jesus Christ. The Bible does not say we should try to scare people out of hell; it tells us to simply share our hope with gentleness.

Second Timothy 2:24 says, "And the Lord's bond-servant must not be quarrelsome, but be kind to all, able to teach, patient when wronged, with gentleness correcting those who are in opposition, if perhaps God may grant them repentance." Again, when we are gentle, we give God the proper atmosphere to work. Gentle men and women are always the most effective soul-winners.

James 3:17 says, "But the wisdom from above is first pure, then peaceable, gentle, reasonable, full of mercy and good fruits, unwavering, without hypocrisy." To speak without gentleness is to speak without the wisdom of God. Proverbs 15:1 advises, "A gentle answer turns away wrath, but a harsh word stirs up anger." It is not the believer who howls the loudest, who sees victory, but the one who is gentle. It is hard to argue with someone who is too gentle to argue back. God is the Good Shepherd, and He leads His sheep and His lambs gently.

Submit yourselves to the Holy Spirit's working out His fruit in you. May we learn that gentleness is not weakness, but rather great strength and a powerful weapon of righteousness.

Chapter 7

The Strength of Joy

Joy is love's strength. Nehemiah 8:10 says, "The joy of the Lord is my strength." Joy is another weapon of righteousness—not just any joy, but the joy of the Lord. In my ongoing vendetta in Christ to destroy the works of the devil, there have been many times when I would have given up were it not for the strengthening I received from the joy of the Lord. Many times when things looked hopeless, I have thought of King David, for the Bible says he "strengthened himself in the Lord his God" (I Sam. 30:6). David was distressed, but the Lord wasn't. Therefore, as he praised his God, David was strengthened, and I have been strengthened many times in the same way.

The Bible says that God's wrath is coming upon the earth, but in spite of this there will be joy in the hearts of those who have put their trust in Him. Psalms 5:10-11 says, "In the multitude of their transgressions thrust them out, for they are rebellious against Thee. But let all who take refuge in Thee be glad, let them ever sing for joy." Psalms 28:7 says, "The Lord is my strength and my shield; my heart trusts in Him, and I am helped; Therefore my heart exalts."

How do we get this joy? Psalms 30:5 tells us, "Weeping may last for the night, but a shout of joy comes in the morning." Joy should fill the heart of every believer who is in right standing before God. Sometimes pain is required to bring us into this right standing. Psalms 51:12 adds, "Restore to me the joy of Thy salvation."

It is not always a pleasant thing to be disciplined by the Lord, but He has promised us that after the sorrow of the discipline, He will restore our joy. If you struggle to understand this concept, it may be because you do not fully understand the scriptual relationship between a father and his son. If you are a blood-bought believer, then you are God's son or daughter, and you can rest assured that He will treat you as His child.

It has been said that if the devil can't steal your joy, he can't keep your goods. Joy is the victorious strength of Christianity. Luke 6:22 says that when men hate us for Christ's sake, we ought to "leap for joy."

God wants His people to be a people of joy. Sad, sorrowful, mournful, depressed, frustrated, and defeated believers are certainly not an uplifting testimony to the greatness of our Heavenly Father.

According to John 15:7-11, those who obey the Father's word will have great joy. Jesus was filled with joy. His cup of joy ran over. In verse 10 Jesus says, "If you keep My commandments, you will abide in My love; just as I have kept My Father's commandments and abide in His love. These things I have spoken to you, that My joy may be in you, and that your joy may be made full." God's word produces joy in the believer, so be filled with His word. Yes, according to Jesus your cup of joy can overflow when you stay in Him, obeying what He has said. Live in His love and you will be filled with His joy. That joy will be a great source of strength—a true weapon of righteousness.

How do you actually get this joy? Well, I got mine when I found out that the Bible says that God is my shield, my helper, my provider, my protector, and my healer. This means that I don't have a worry; I am never alone. I don't have to be afraid, because my relationship with Him as His child has produced great joy. I am God's beloved son!

The joy of a believer will attract those who are lost faster than anything. Joyful people stand out in the crowd in this depressing hour. Satan cannot defeat a truly joy-filled Christian.

Like the other fruit of the Holy Spirit, joy is the product of our personal relationship with the Father, Son and Holy Spirit. This is the only place where true joy can be found. All other providers of joy will only be temporary at best.

Notes

Chapter 8

The Weapon of Goodness

God is love, and God is good. The goodness of God is the essence of God's character. Because He is love, He is of necessity good; for love is what makes a person good. The fruit of goodness is a mighty weapon of righteousness.

Ephesians 5:1 says, "Therefore be imitators of God, as beloved children; and walk in love, just as Christ also loved you, and gave Himself up for us." Galatians five and Ephesians five have something in common: they both describe the fruit of the Holy Spirit, and they both list the works of the flesh. In both of these chapters, Paul tells us not to be partakers of those who tell their dirty jokes and live immoral and impure lives. "Bad company corrupts good manners." He tells us that though we were formerly in darkness, now we are in the light and should "walk as children of light" (Ephesians 5:7-8).

In Ephesians 5:12, Paul says that it is disgraceful even to speak of the things practiced by those in darkness. Those fellowshipping with goodness have no business talking about those dirty things, let alone being entertained by them. What does the goodness of God have to do with the PG, PG-13, R and X rated things of the television set? This entertainment of darkness has stolen more from the believer's personal intimacy with Christ than nearly anything else. Murder, immorality, rape, theft, swearing, drugs, and alcohol—these are the things of darkness. What do these things have in common with goodness?

Paul says in Romans 15:13, "Now may the God of hope fill you with all joy and peace in believing." Do you have joy and peace in believing? He then continues, "That you may abound in hope by the power of the Holy Spirit. And concerning you, my brethren, I myself also am convinced that you yourselves are full of goodness, filled with all knowledge, and able also to admonish one another." Paul is pleased with them because they are full of goodness.

In Romans 15:2, Paul admonishes, "Let each one of us please his neighbor for his good." The neighbor's good, he wrote, not our own good. As he explains, "For even Christ did not please Himself" (vs. 3). Jesus did everything that He did for our good, not His own. I believe the Bible is telling us that we ought to be like Jesus. He is good to us, and He expects us to likewise be good to one another. He carried our weaknesses and has told us to carry the weakness of our brothers. Good, Christ like Believers are truly their brother's keeper. Goodness is the quality that looks out for its neighbor first; it looks out for those who are weak. As we begin to put others first, we will find that we will have more than enough provisions to meet our every need.

Romans 13:3 says, "For rulers are not a cause of fear for good behavior, but for evil." The authorities of this world, whether human or spiritual, have no leverage against those who do good.

Let me now show you how goodness becomes a mighty weapon against the works of the devil. In Romans 12:20-21 Paul writes, "But if your enemy is hungry, feed him, and if he is thirsty, give him a drink; for in so doing you will heap burning coals upon his head. Do not be overcome by evil, but overcome evil with good." There it is. Overcome evil with good. And in Romans 20:19 Paul says, "Vengeance is Mine, I will repay, says the Lord." In other words, you do good and I will come and take vengeance. Wow! Talk about power! Goodness sets you up so that God will fight in your behalf.

When we try to fight evil with evil, we put ourselves on evil's level; we stay the hand of God. But God will actually fight for us when we operate in goodness. In John 10:11, Jesus said, "I am the good shepherd; the good shepherd lays down His life for the sheep." Goodness puts everybody else ahead of oneself, even ones enemies. And this godly character trait brings on the scene He who is wholly good. Goodness is truly a weapon of righteousness, and it commands great power.

When the fruit of goodness develops in our lives through the Holy Spirit, we will become like our Father, because only He is truly good. When we start to put others first, we will see many come to Christ by our witness of goodness. Let each of us make a conscious effort to submit to the Holy Spirit and allow Him to work in our lives to bring forth this great quality of Christ in us.

Notes

Chapter 9

The Consistent Power of Faithfulness

Faith and Faithfulness is love's confidence. It is trust not just in believing, but also in the faithfulness of our work. James 2:17,18 says "Even so faith, if it has no works, is dead, being by itself." But someone may well say, "you have faith, and I have works; show me your faith without the works, and I will show you my faith by my works." Jesus Christ is our faithful High Priest. He is always faithful in desiring and fulfilling the will of His Father. We should know by now that it is the mission of the Holy Spirit to transform us into the character of Jesus; to bring forth the fruit of the Holy Spirit in the life of every believer.

Writing to the Colossians, Paul told them to be sure to put on the "new man." Colossians 3:12-15 says, "And so, as those who have been chosen of God, holy and beloved, put on a heart of compassion, kindness, humility, gentleness and patience; bearing with one another, and forgiving each other, whoever has a complaint against anyone; just as the Lord forgave you, so also should you forgive. And beyond all these things put on love, which is the perfect bond of unity. And let the peace of Christ rule in your hearts, to which indeed you were called in one body; and be thankful."

This description is opposite of what the world considers to be strength. There is no "dog-eat-dog" attitude in Paul's words. The chosen of God, through the fruit of the Holy Spirit, can stand up in holiness with the weapons of light, face the devil, face death, and face disaster square in the eye and say, "I win! You are defeated! Christ has made it so, and I am reminding you of the fact." Confidence abides in the heart of those who are faithful. They are as bold as a lion. Stand up believer, and gird yourself with the fruit of light. Walk out onto the stage of life in the character and power of the One Who is now living His life through your body, which is His temple.

Romans 6:12-13 says, "Therefore do not let sin reign in your mortal body that you should obey its lust, and do not go on presenting the members of your body to sin as instruments of unrighteousness; but present yourselves to God as those alive from the dead, and your members as instruments of righteousness to God."

Believer, you are a temple of the Holy Spirit. When that becomes a reality to you, then you will begin to understand the ultimate goal of all sickness and disease and all satanic attacks. The arch enemy of Christ is out to destroy His temple. As I began to understand this spiritual truth more clearly, I began to pray for the sick differently. I saw sickness and disease and every other attack as warfare against God's temple. When praying for believers, I would command in

Jesus' name that these enemies detach themselves from the temple of the Holy Spirit and go to a deserted place. Since I began praying this way, I have seen a dramatic rise in healing taking place. Remember though, it is the faithful who have true confidence. This confidence is simply a trust in our Father.

Those who put on the new man, the fruit of the Holy Spirit, will find themselves about their Father's business. The weapons of righteousness are the greatest tools the Holy Spirit has given to God's sons and daughters to empower them to succeed in their spiritual work.

Romans 6:16 says, "Do you not know that when you present yourselves to someone as slaves for obedience, you are slaves to the one whom you obey, either of sin resulting in death, or of obedience resulting in righteousness?" If you obey the voice of money, sex or power, you are a slave of lust. Notice I said if you obey the voice of money, sex and power. These can be great blessings from God but we are to control them, they are not to control us. We are to be controlled (totally submitted) only by the Holy Spirit. Verses 17 and 18 say, "But thanks be to God that though you were slaves of sin, you became obedient from the heart to that form of teaching to which you were committed, and having been freed from sin, you became slaves of righteousness." In essence Paul is saying, "Do you remember how you used to give yourselves to sin? Well, in the same way, now give yourselves to righteousness."

God and His word are ever faithful, and they can always be counted on. They will lead you on the pathway of truth and righteousness everyday. Even when we have failed over and over again, our Father remains faithful; His word remains forever settled. God is the same yesterday, today and forever. His covenant with us is the same yesterday, today and forever.

I am amazed by how many preachers there are who recognize that God has not changed toward salvation; yet they think He has changed in many other areas, especially the area of supernatural manifestation. The root of their error is that they have not truly accepted the unwavering faithfulness of God and His covenant. Simply put, no Christian can receive anything from God except it comes through the blood covenant of Christ, and that covenant has never changed. Men's theologies and philosophies have changed, but our faithful Heavenly Father, His Son Jesus Christ, and His covenant have never changed. Jesus is still doing what He has always done for those who believe.

We need this fruit of faithfulness in our lives. You may be very talented, but if you are not faithful it has no ultimate value. A few years ago I had one of the best guitar players I had ever heard on our worship team. Unfortunately, he was not very faithful. Sometimes he would show up for practice and other times he would not. I spoke to him about his unfaithfulness, but he didn't see it that way. He knew he was better than the rest of the band and therefore did not require as much practice. I told him that even if that was so, the practice was not just for ourselves; it was for the benefit of all. It was in the unity of the group that his unfaithfulness took its toll. Even though he was the best, I had no choice but to remove him. His talent without faithfulness had no value to our program. This can be true not only for musicians, but for Sunday school teachers, ushers, nursery workers, deacons, and every believer. One of the things we lack in the Church today is faithfulness, all the way from tithing to attendance. It weakens the Church into an impotent, ineffective body.

The Scripture says that if we are faithful in small things, then God will entrust us with larger things. Faithfulness is the key to spiritual growth. Talents can be taught and developed, but faithfulness comes from the Holy Spirit. It is His fruit.

I am where I am today because I've been faithful with my love for God, with my tithe, and with my attendance to church meetings. Make no mistake: God hasn't paid me a wage for my faithfulness. But He has entrusted me with bigger and better spiritual things.

When I was a young Christian, I ministered early every Sunday morning in a large nursing home. My wife and I led several to Christ there. The administrator told us that of all those who came there to minister, we had the best attendance. Why? Because these old folks could depend on us to be there on time with a word of encouragement and love. We were faithful, and God worked through our faithfulness.

In the factory ministry I was also faithful. I anointed the sick with motor oil and prayed for them. My life was a faithful witness. I shared Christ with hundreds of people in the two years I was there. And, I might add, I was also faithful by excelling in the quality and quantity of my work.

In the bus ministry we were also faithful. The kids could count on my wife and me visiting them on Saturday and being on time to pick them up on Sunday. God did the rest. The bus was always full.

Psalms 31:23 says, "O love the Lord, all you His godly ones! The Lord preserves the faithful." Proverbs 12:22 sums up my desire, "Lying lips are an abomination to the Lord, but those who deal faithfully are His delight." My heart's cry is that my Father would be delighted in me. This is the reason I have sought for the fruit of faithfulness. Lying lips are the lips of those who have committed themselves to do a thing and then be unfaithful to see it through. The book of Ephesians is addressed to "the faithful in Christ Jesus" (vs. 1:1). When writing to Timothy, Paul told him to entrust his teachings to "faithful men" (II Tim. 2:2), for they were the only ones that could be trusted to carry on the spreading of the gospel of Christ.

Divorce is the ultimate result of unfaithfulness to the marriage vows. A man is no better than his word. To be faithful means saying what you mean and meaning what you say.

Many parents have children who continually misbehave simply because they have not been faithful to their word. They say, "Johnny, I'll spank you if you do that again." Then Johnny does it again but doesn't get the promised spanking—only more "promises." From that point on, Johnny will take every word from that parent with a grain of salt. Then the parents wonder where Johnny went astray. He went astray due to the unfaithful words of his own parents.

Revelation 2:10 says, "Be faithful unto death, and I will give you the crown of life." Be faithful, beloved, all the way to eternity in everything you have set your hand to do. If you are going to start, don't stop. If you are going to stop, don't start. Be faithful.

Notes

Chapter 10

The Battle Zone of Self-Control

Self-control is love's victory. There can be no victory in the life of a Christian whose flesh is always standing in the way of the move of the Holy Spirit. Self-control is simply setting self aside so that the ministry of Christ can go forth. Whatever needs to be set aside must be set aside; the ministry of the gospel must not be discredited, stopped or even slowed down.

Self-control is setting aside our desires, our passions, and our appetites. The lack of self-control is more evident in some things than others. For example, sometimes the obese believer's lack of self-control is much more evident than the believer who hides his cigarettes or his can of beer. But you do not have to be obese to lack self-control in your eating. Many thin people overeat. You see them at the buffet bar pigging out, trying to eat twenty dollars worth of food for three ninety-five. Self-control is keeping the carnal desires of self in check.

One of the hardest self-control battles is our thought life. The mind is undoubtedly the devil's battlefield; and self-control plays a big part in winning this battle. When wrong thoughts come along, there are two choices available: We can either entertain the thought or cast it out. The Bible says, "The weapons of our warfare are not of the flesh, but divinely powerful for the destruction of fortresses. We are destroying speculations and every lofty thing raised up against the knowledge of God, and we are taking every thought captive to the obedience of Christ" (II Corinthians 10:4-5).

Wrong thoughts are often very appealing to the man of flesh. I have learned that when the flesh man likes something, lookout. Sin is right around the corner. All wrong thoughts do not necessarily come from demonic powers, since according to Matthew 15:19, "Out of the heart come evil thoughts."

God's people need to keep their hearts pure, for it is "the pure in heart" who will see God. Self-control plays an important part in this warfare of the mind. It is the strength of a believer's self-control that makes the determination as to how long wrong thoughts will be tolerated.

Allow me to expose a demonic scheme in this war of the mind that many believers fall prey to. The enemy comes along with his evil or dirty thought and plants it in your mind. You respond as a man or woman of God and throw it out. At that moment you think you have won the battle, but look out! Here comes the counter-attack. The enemy returns within seconds and says, "Boy, you sure are a lousy Christian for having that kind of thought." The devil is both the tempter and the accuser. Don't be afraid to tell the enemy you are a man or a woman of God, and that those dirty thoughts are his and not yours. He is a liar and the Father of it.

The fruit of self-control will not allow you to imagine anything you desire or look upon anything you want to see or hear anything you want to hear.

Self-control of our mouths is very important as well. Proverbs 17:28 says, "Even a fool, when he keeps silent, is considered wise." You can't tell a fool is a fool as long as he is silent. We wouldn't stick our feet in our mouths nearly so often if we exercised self-control of our mouths. More unbelievers are turned off to Jesus Christ because of the uncontrolled mouths of believers than perhaps from all the plans of the enemy.

We need to exercise self-control over our feelings and emotions, too. There is nothing inherently wrong with feelings and emotions; God gave them to us. But they were not intended to control us. The time that I have been misled the most, from buying a car to judging a man's character, have been when I've been strongly influenced by my feelings or emotions.

Continuation of self-control

Self cannot produce self-control. Second Corinthians 5:14 says, "For the love of Christ controls us." The love of Christ is what produces true spiritual self-control. It is a fruit of the Holy Spirit, not some kind of self-imposed asceticism. When we allow the love of Christ to control us, then we will no longer walk after the flesh but after the Spirit.

Self-control is discipline of the self. The discipline that leads toward outward holiness begins with the Word of God. Paul said, "All scripture is inspired by God and profitable for teaching, for reproof, for correction, for training in righteousness" (II Timothy 3:16).

Scripture will train us or discipline us in doing righteousness. It is by willing, prayerful and persistent obedience to the Scriptures that godly patterns are developed in our lives.

Every Christian who makes progress in holiness is a person who has disciplined his life so that he spends time every day in prayer, worship and Bible study. The person who is progressing in holiness may fail in his efforts many times, but he doesn't quit. As for me, I am never down. I am either up or getting up. Proverbs 24:16 says, "For a righteous man falls seven times, and rises again." God wants us to persevere in discipline toward increasing holiness.

Ask your Heavenly Father to help you grow up into the image of Jesus and that His character would be manifested in your life. Set your self aside, that Christ may live in and through you. In Him you can do it!

Chapter 11
Patience and Kindness

Patience is extremely important for a believer to develop. If a believer, or even an unbeliever, desires to improve his or her self in a particular area of their life; be it a change in attitude, habits, a skill or whatever, there must be first the desire to change, then the will or determination to change, and finally the patience to see it accomplished. To be an achiever you need to have the desire and the will to do a thing, and then the patience to see yourself through it. Now desire and determination are not a fruit of the spirit, but rather a work of the spirit, but patience is a fruit of the spirit, and a very necessary fruit for anyone who wishes to accomplish a thing.

Some people have patience and they may not even be a Christian. This would be a good character trait, but nothing good or bad is acceptable to God unless it comes by way of the shed blood of Jesus Christ. On the other hand, a believer most certainly should have this fruit showing in their Christian walk. As the believer grows, the evidence of the fruit of patience, along with the other fruit of the spirit will be seen in their life.

Patience is love's waiting. Isaiah 40:31 says, "Yet those who wait for the Lord will gain strength; they will mount up with wings like eagles, they will run and not get tired, they will walk and not become weary."

It is in our time of waiting before the Lord that our strength is renewed. This patient waiting upon the Lord ought to be a daily thing, not just something you do because you're about to become totally exhausted. Battle fatigue is a big killer in a war, but those that rest and patiently wait upon the Lord shall have their strength renewed. Stressed-out and burned-out believers are those who have fatigued themselves by not waiting on the Lord until they are renewed and strengthened. This patient waiting will be a quality in you that will not surrender to circumstances, situations or symptoms. Patience keeps its eye on reaching the mark. Patience will keep your faith applied while the Word is at work in your behalf. Patience, Self-Control and Kindness are all closely related to each other. You need self-control to have patience and then kindness comes out of patience. There are a great many people that we find ourselves having trouble being kind to; because of their appearance, their behavior and actions. Kindness cannot come forth if we are not patient with people.

James 5:7-8 says, "Behold, the farmer waits for the precious produce of the soil, being patient about it, until it gets the early and late rains. You too be patient; strengthen your hearts, for the coming of the Lord is at hand." Just as the farmer waits for the produce of the soil, we should wait for all those whom Christ died for. Vine's Expository Dictionary of New

Testament Words states, that the noun in Greek for kindness is *Philalthropia*, for philos, loving, anthropos, man. In laymen terms kindness is simply loving man. In Titus 3:4 *Philanthropia*, speaking of the kindness of God, is translated "His love toward man". Our kindness is our expression of our love.

The six Greek words that can be translated kind or kindness can also be translated as Better, Easy, Good, Goodness, Gracious, Gentleness, Pleasant, Love, and Courteous. Kindness is certainly a fruit of the Holy spirit. Only He can produce this attitude and behavior in us toward all people at all times.

Kindness was a very strong character trait of the Lord Jesus. He was kind to all men, even those in great darkness. This was possible with Him as it is with us. In His personal relationship with His Father, He understood that by God's grace all men could be changed. All of us at some time or other have been unlovely; thank God for His grace and kindness in those times.

Prov. 19:22 says, "what is desirable in a man, is his kindness." One of the greatest characteristics of a Christian man or woman is their kindness: a man will be remembered more for his kindness than perhaps for anything else.

First Corinthians 13:4 says, "Love is patient, Love is kind," Ephesians 4:32 says, "be kind to one another," II Timothy 2:24 says, "but be kind to all."

Peace and Calm rests upon the man of kindness, he does not respond to people in anger. I say to my children, "don't get so hyper, be kind to each other," there is a peace and calm in that. In this peace and calm is where you can hear that still small voice of

God. Kindness makes the giver and the receiver feel like very important people. Ephesians 4:32 says, "And be kind to one another, tender hearted, forgiving each other, just as God in Christ also has forgiven you."

Chapter 12

Jesus-Breathed Power Is Forgiveness

John 20:21-23 says, "Jesus therefore said to them again, 'Peace be with you; as the Father has sent Me, I also send you.' And when He said this, He breathed on them, and said to them, 'Receive the Holy Spirit. If you forgive the sins of any, their sins have been forgiven them; if you retain the sins of any, they have been retained.'"

A companion to this verse is found in Matthew 18:18. In this verse Jesus tells His disciples, "Truly I say to you, whatever you shall bind on earth shall be bound in heaven; and whatever you loose on earth shall be loosed in heaven."

The ministry of Jesus Christ was to extend forgiveness so that men could be reconciled unto God and to one another. This same ministry has been given to the Church today. Remember, Jesus said, "As the Father has sent Me, I also send you."

A few within the Church have not understood some important facets of the Church's ministry. I want to give those precious believers the message of forgiveness and the power it has to release those who are held captive by their sins and their hurts. I want to address particularly those who have been damaged by sins committed against them. Only forgiveness can bring healing to a wounded spirit.

There are many wounded believers within the Church of Jesus Christ, and there are many that have been wounded and have left the Church. This wounding of the spirit comes from many places—husbands wounding wives, wives wounding husbands, parents wounding children, believers wounding believers, pastors wounding congregations, congregations wounding pastors, in-laws wounding inlaws, and on and on. Death wounds. Adultery wounds. Divorce wounds.

The cries of pain and blame are heard by ministers day after day:

"My mother didn't treat me right."

"My father did me wrong."

"My husband died too early."

"My brother greatly offended me."

"The preacher directed his sermon toward me."

"A sister gossiped about me."

"I was molested as a young child."

"I was raped and it destroyed my life."

I'm not saying bad things aren't bad. Certainly they are. The pain is real. The hurt is deep. But as believers in the One who heals wounded spirits, we cannot allow our wounds to control us the rest of our lives.

Proverbs 18:14 says, "The spirit of man can endure his sickness, but a broken spirit who can bear?" The human spirit is a powerful force. If it is healthy and strong, it can carry us through times of wounding, sores, festering cuts and abrasions, and bruises, whether physical, emotional or mental. An emotional or mental wound can be much more deadly than a physical wound. But Jesus has offered us total healing.

Many of us have come for prayer to be released from the hurt, torment and pain of inner wounds; yet within two days the same hurt has returned. If the spirit that is to sustain you in your time of hurt is wounded, it has no strength to sustain you.

A wounded spirit cannot be carried, though many believers try. Wounds hurt. When there is something inside that really hurts, this hurt is manifested in our lives and in our relationships with other people. The hurt is real! But let's see how we can get rid of this hurt once and for all.

One of our problems is that most of us have been well trained to fake it. We fight like cats and dogs all the way to church, then we walk in the church door so holy and dignified; everyone thinks we are the perfect Christian family. Then on the way home all hell breaks loose again. We are professional fakes. We say, "Good morning, my dear sister. It's so good to see you." Then we whisper, "You old hag; I remember what you said about my darling children." We are fake.

How come we don't fight on Monday morning like we do on Sunday morning? We get up and send the kids off to secular schools so they can get A's in everything that we as Christians are diametrically opposed to. A lot of folks don't even come to church on Wednesday nights so the kids can get more rest, so they will be able to learn more of the things we are opposed to. We've got things mixed up, don't you think? We say to the kids, "You get up to your bedroom until you learn how to act. You go to your room until you get some manners." I wonder what parents think is in that bedroom to teach them manners.

Proverbs 17:22 says, "A joyful heart is good medicine, but a broken spirit dries up the bones." Our body replenishes itself with new cells every seven years; yet scientists can't figure out why we keep aging. Science doesn't have all the answers and neither does psychology. I don't believe we have to dig up all the garbage of yesterday to get healing today.

Even some "Christian psychologists" would have you go back to the time your father molested you and relive it. Then they would have you imagine Jesus standing in the corner watching so you can receive some kind of inner healing. I say, "HOGWASH!" We have God's word to heal us. And the Word says, "A broken spirit dries up the bones."

What is inside bones? Marrow. What does marrow do? Make blood. What does blood carry? Life. Leviticus 17:11 says, "For the life of the flesh is in the blood." A broken, wounded, defiled spirit dries up your life; it cuts off the flow of life to you. You begin to die on the inside.

Let's see where this wounded spirit comes from. In Mark 7:15, Jesus said, "There is nothing outside the man which going into him can defile him; but the things which proceed out of the man are what defile the man." Nothing on the outside—no experience, no hurt, no wound—nothing from the outside can defile us. Only what comes out from the inside. We need to guard our hearts, beloved, for out of our hearts flow the issues of life (Prov. 4:23).

As long as we are in this world, things will continue to come against us. You would have to live in an isolated, padded room to avoid things coming against you. But that is not what wounds and defiles you; it is the way you respond. It is whether you are willing to forgive and forget. It is what comes out of your heart that does the defiling, not what comes out of someone else's heart. Jesus said this is so. If you will receive this and apply it to your life, you can be forever free.

The Greek word translated "defile" means "to make unfit for holy purposes." It is not what comes from the outside that will make you unfit for holy purposes, only that which comes from within your own heart. Those with a wounded, hurt and defiled spirit are disqualified for holy purposes. If we have allowed ourselves to get into this condition, we cannot be used for holy purposes. The wounded spirit disqualifies us. We must get rid of it and receive our healing once and for all.

The decision to be healed is yours. Do you really want to be healed? If you do, you will have to forgive and forget, never to recall or rehash it again.

I want to be fit for holy purposes. Some of you who are reading this have been called into the ministry, and you know it. But your holy purpose can't be fulfilled because you have been disqualified. Well, glory to God! Let's get qualified again! The gifts and callings of God are never taken away; we just disqualify ourselves.

The apostle Paul was mistreated severely, far worse than any of us. He was beaten, wounded, tortured, mocked, cursed, and lied about; yet he never became unfit for holy purposes. Why? Because every time the offense and the wound came, he said, "Father, forgive them. I forgive them. Oh, Father, they don't even know what they are doing."

When you release a man or woman of their sin against you, you release yourself from the power of your own hurt. Let me say that again: When you release a man or woman from their sin against you, you release yourself from the imprisoning power of your own hurt!

According to John 20:22-21, as sons and daughters of God, we have the authority to release others and thereby release ourselves from our hurts. If we won't release others, we disqualify ourselves from being fit for holy purposes. Remember that one of the highest holy purposes of God is the ministry of reconciliation.

"Oh, he hurt me," you say. No, it was not what he did but how you responded that did the damage. You should have released him immediately through forgiveness. Then you would have also released yourself from the pain. Before we read this passage of Scripture (John 13:37-14:3), I want to encourage you that God does love you, He is for you not against you. May we see in this passage that even when Peter denied the Lord that God still loved him and was making wonderful provisions for him. Each of us have denied the Lord in one way or another, but it is important for you to receive your forgiveness and jump-up and go again. As we read this passage remember the original had no chapter marking in the middle. Jesus answered, "Will you lay down your life for Me? Truly, truly, I say to you, a cock shall not crow, until you deny Me three times. Let not your heart be troubled; believe in God, believe also in Me. In my Father's house are many dwelling places; if it were not so, I would have told you; for I go and prepare a place for you. And if I go and prepare a place for you, I will come again, and receive you to Myself; that where I am, there you may be also." Oh, Beloved, do you see the love, forgiveness and compassion of God toward those who are His. Even in the midst of your denial He is making beautiful plans for you. Turn your hearts, children, back to your Father who loves you so much. Forgive—it's God's way!

Do you hear the Holy Spirit? He is calling you right now to release those who have sinned against you and receive your healing. Begin to call out the names of those who have sinned against you. Call out their names and forgive them forever. You'll begin to feel pure, clean and undefiled. You have the power to release both them and yourself; use it!

Some husbands and wives need to release each other. You say, "But I don't want to forgive. He is guilty. She is guilty." You alone have the authority to release your spouse and thereby release yourself. If you will not forgive, then you will retain. If the light that is in you is darkness, oh, how great is that darkness! Forgive and be healed. The weapons of righteousness are truly awesome. God's ways are so much higher and wiser than ours.

As we allow the Holy Spirit to produce the character of Jesus Christ in us, personally and individually, then we will begin to see a new and victorious life come forth—a life of power and authority with all purity, goodness and gentleness. We will discover the real Christian life of love, joy and peace. We'll see the latter rain power of the Holy Spirit rise up in believers as they stand firm with the weapons of righteousness—the right hand to attack and the left hand to defend.

Beloved, unforgiveness is the biggest roadblock to spiritual maturity and spiritual manifestations in your behalf. Let us "receive the Holy Spirit." The Holy Spirit is God. Say it out loud. The Holy Spirit is God. He lives within me, and He desires to transform me into the image of Jesus Christ.

Chapter 13

Warrior Sons and Daughters of God

Only the true sons and daughters of God are capable of holding up the weapons of righteousness; only they can wield a power so glorious and awesome that it can tear down satanic strongholds and set captives free.

Ephesians 1:3-5 says, "Blessed be the God and Father of our Lord Jesus Christ, who has blessed us with every spiritual blessing in the heavenly places in Christ, just as He chose us in Him before the foundation of the world, that we should be holy and blameless before Him. In love He predestined us to adoption as sons through Jesus Christ Himself, according to the kind intention of His will."

From before the foundation of the world, God predestined us to adoption as sons through Jesus Christ. John 1:12 says, "As many as received Him, to them He gave the right to become children of God, even to those who believe in His name." Verse 13 goes on to say that these have not been "born of blood, nor of the will of the flesh, nor of the will of man, but of God."

Those who receive Christ are born again by the Spirit of God and are placed in the standing of adopted sons. According to Galatians 4:5-7, this is "that we might receive the adoption as sons. And because you are sons, God has sent forth the Spirit of His Son into our hearts, crying, 'Abba! Father!' Therefore, you are no longer a slave, but a son; and if a son, then an heir through God." Beloved, if you have received Christ, you are now the Father's son. Jesus Christ was the firstborn, and He is not ashamed to call you His brother or sister.

As sons of God the Holy Spirit is bringing forth in each of us the character of Jesus Christ. It is this very character of Christ in us that will result in sons of God that are about their Father's business. What is that business? To destroy the works of darkness and set those held captive free. In the Father's business then, the weapons of righteousness are the ultimate fighting force. It is the fruit of light that flashes forth from His sons and daughters that will be the light that leads many to safety.

Raise up your swords, sons of God, and proclaim in the character of Christ that we shall be more than conquerors, to the glory of the Lamb and the saints of God.

If you are not a child of God, do not despair, for you can be if you want to be. Right where you are just say, "Jesus, I receive you as my Savior. Thank you for dying for my sin. Jesus, because you rose from the grave with all power I can be born again into God's family. Thank you, my Lord. Amen."

If you have received Christ, write us. We will be so glad to hear from you.

May the love, joy, peace and grace of God be upon each of you in your journey as a son or daughter of the heavenly Father, armed with the weapons of righteousness for the left hand and the right, going forth to destroy the works of the devil.

Notes

Summary

Let your eyes look directly ahead, and let your gaze be fixed straight in front of you. Watch the path of your feet, and all your ways will be established, Do not turn to the right nor to the left; turn your foot from evil (Proverbs 4:25-27).

As we strive toward the mark of the high calling of Jesus Christ, let us remember that the Christian life is never free from mistakes. We have all made mistakes and we will make them again and again. But as Charles Allen once pointed out, the difference between a sheep and a pig is this; when a sheep falls in a mudhole, it bleats to get out. When a pig falls in, he just lies there and wallows. You may have fallen in your quest to be like Jesus but Beloved get up and start again.

If you will submit to the work that the Holy Spirit is doing in you, you can be sure that the work He has begun He will bring to a completion in Christ Jesus. So allow and even invite the Father to prune your tree so that the Fruit of the Character of Christ may grow in abundance in your life.

Allow me to put into my own words what Jesus said in John 15, "You didn't choose Me!, I chose you! I appointed you to go and produce lovely fruit, so that no matter what you ask for from the Father, using My name, He will give it to you." I hope you can see how the fruit of the Holy Spirit in your life will release answered prayer, power and provisions for you and those you minister to.

I am on a highway that goes the distance and on this highway there is no darkness only light, please come and go with me. You don't know the way?, you may say. Jesus is the only way. I invite you, if you have not already done so, to join me on the road to God with Jesus Christ. I urge you to do it now.

About the Author

Alden Reed is a pastor and evangelist. He and his wife Connie have six children. Pastor Reed is a graduate of Lester Sumrall's World Harvest Bible College. He also studied for two years under Morris Cerullo's ministry.

Pastor Reed has had a weekly television program in 1991 and has appeared with Lester Sumrall and on other Christian programs.

Pastor Reed's revelation of the Weapons of Righteousness has been taught by him at Norval Hayes' New Life Bible College in Cleveland, Tennessee. He has proclaimed this revelation from California to Connecticut, and from Mexico to Michigan. Pastor Reed's desire is to see believers rise up in the Spirit of Jesus and raze the foundations of hell, going in and setting free those held captive.

If you are interested in hosting a conference or crusade on the Weapons of Righteousness in your geographical area, please contact us for more information at the following address:

        New Life Church, Ministries
        P.O. Box 96
        Tarboro, North Carolina 27886

If you would like to make arrangements for speaking engagements, or to order additional copies of The Weapons of Righteousness, please write to the following address:

>Reverend Alden Reed
>P.O. Box 96
>Tarboro, N.C. 27886
>Phone 919-823-7949

The cost of The Weapons of Righteousness is	$5.95
Shipping and handling cost is	1.25
	$7.10

This is excellent Sunday school quarterly material. Reduced cost for Sunday school orders.

Notes

Notes